MALLET CHORD STUDIES

Chord Voicings and Arpeggio Patterns for Vibraphone and Marimba and Other Instruments

by Emil Richards

CONTENTS

ISBN 978-1-4234-6991-9

HAL•LEONARD®
CORPORATION
7777 W. BLUEMOUND RD. P.O. BOX 13819 MILWAUKEE, WI 53213

In Australia Contact:
Hal Leonard Australia Pty. Ltd.
4 Lentara Court
Cheltenham, Victoria, 3192 Australia
Email: ausadmin@halleonard.com.au

Visit Hal Leonard Online at
www.halleonard.com

OPEN FOUR-MALLET CHORDS
Major 6th Chords

Closed Position

Formula for Open Positions

Open Positions

Write out and play open Major 6th Chords in all keys. Note that C 6th has the very same notes as A minor 7th. Find and identify the minor 7th chord for every major 6th chord.

OPEN FOUR-MALLET CHORDS
Minor 6th Chords

Closed Position

Formula for Open Positions

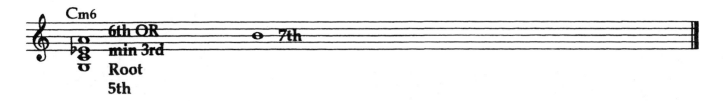

Open Positions

Write out and play open minor 6th Chords in all keys.

OPEN FOUR-MALLET CHORDS
Major 7th Chords

Closed Positions

Formula for Open Positions

Open Positions

Write out and play open Major 7th chords in all keys.

MAJOR 7th EXERCISE

SHORT MAJOR 7th EXERCISE

OPEN FOUR-MALLET CHORDS
Major 7th (–3) Chords

Closed Position

Formula for Open Positions

Major 7th
m 3rd
Root
5th

Open Positions

Write out and play open Major 7th/minor 3rd chords in all keys.

MAJOR 7th (–3) EXERCISE

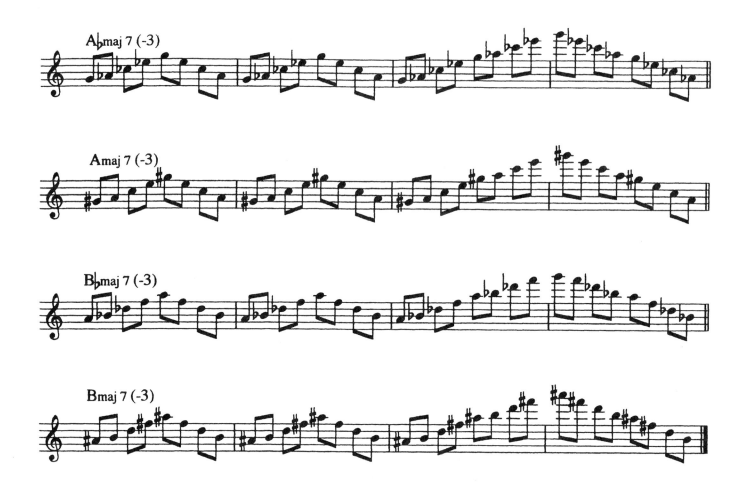

SHORT MAJOR 7th (–3) EXERCISE

OPEN FOUR-MALLET CHORDS
Major 7th (+5) Chords

Closed Positions

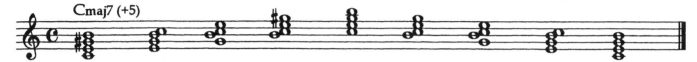

Formula for Open Positions

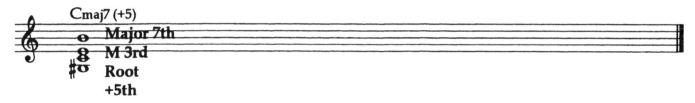

Open Positions

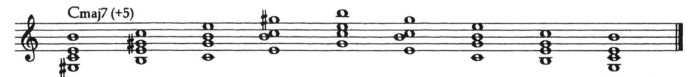

Write out and play open Major 7th/Augmented Chords in all keys.

MAJOR 7th (+5) EXERCISE

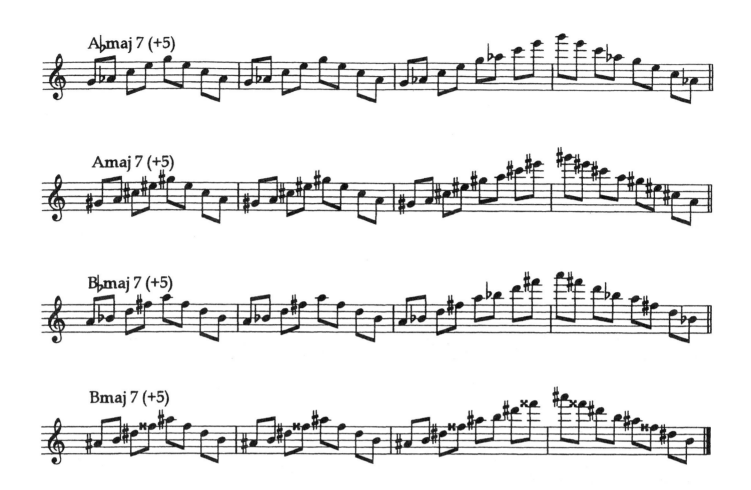

SHORT MAJOR 7th (+5) EXERCISE

OPEN FOUR-MALLET CHORDS
Dominant 7th Chords

Closed Position

Formula for Open Positions

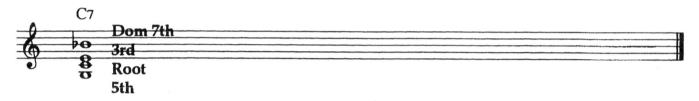

Open Positions

Write out and play open Dominant 7th Chords in all keys.

DOMINANT 7th EXERCISE

SHORT DOMINANT 7th EXERCISE

OPEN FOUR-MALLET CHORDS
Diminished 7th Chords

Closed Position

Formula for Open Positions

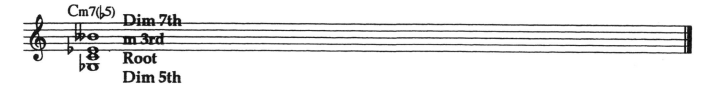

Open Positions

Write out and play open Diminished 7th Chords in all keys. Note that C Dim7, Eb Dim7, Gb Dim 7, and A Dim7 have all the same notes in the chords. You will find when you write them out, that there are only three different Diminished 7th's. The others are just inversions of those three.

OPEN FOUR-MALLET CHORDS
Minor 7th Chords

Closed Position

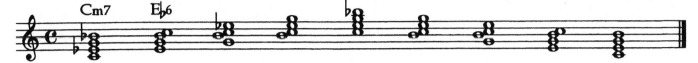

Formula for Open Positions

Open Positions

Write out and play open minor 7th Chords in all keys. Note that Cm 7th has the very same notes as Eb 6th. Find and identify the Major 6th for every minor 7th chord.

MINOR 7th EXERCISE

22

SHORT MINOR 7th EXERCISE

OPEN FOUR-MALLET CHORDS
Minor 7th (–5) Chords

Closed Position

Formula for Open Positions

Open Positions

Write out and play open minor 7th/-5 Chords in all keys.

MINOR 7th (−5) EXERCISE

26

SHORT MINOR 7th (−5) EXERCISE

OPEN FOUR-MALLET CHORDS
7th (Sus 4) Chords

Closed Position

Formula for Open Positions

Open Positions

Write out and play open 7th (Sus 4) Chords in all keys.

7th (SUS 4) EXERCISE

SHORT 7th (SUS 4) EXERCISE

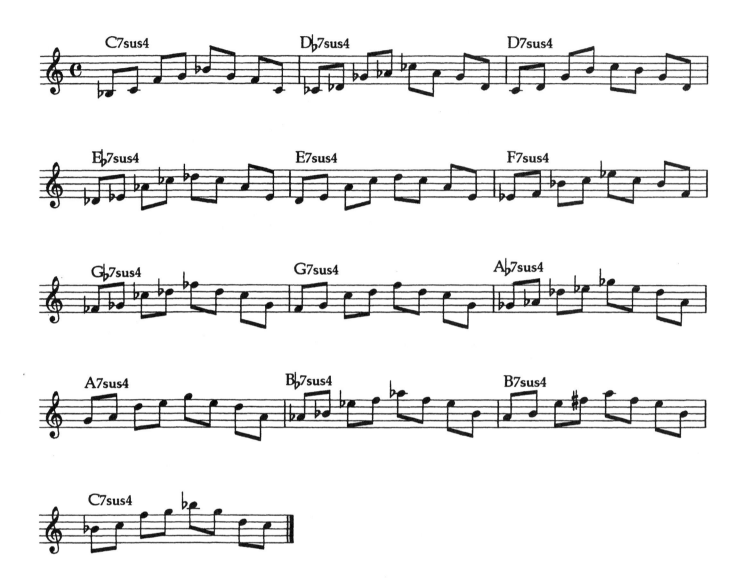

OPEN FOUR-MALLET CHORDS
Augmented 7th Chords

Closed Position

Formula for Open Positions

Open Positions

Write out and play open Augmented 7th Chords in all keys.

AUGMENTED 7th EXERCISE

SHORT AUGMENTED 7th EXERCISE

9th CHORDS

DOMINANT 7th (+11) EXERCISE

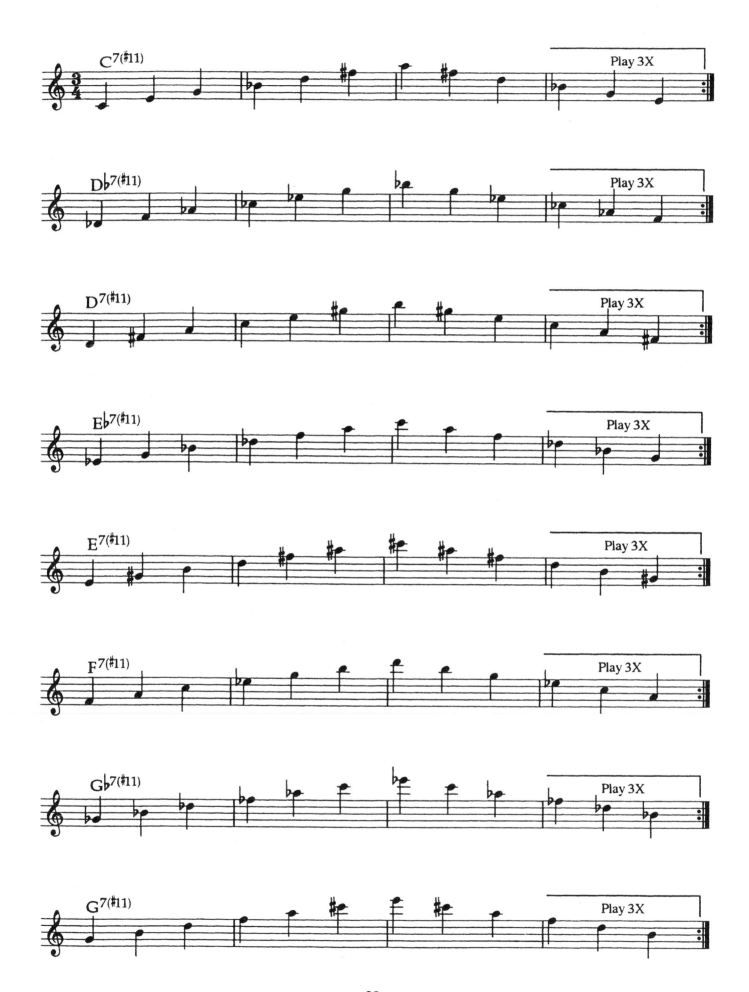

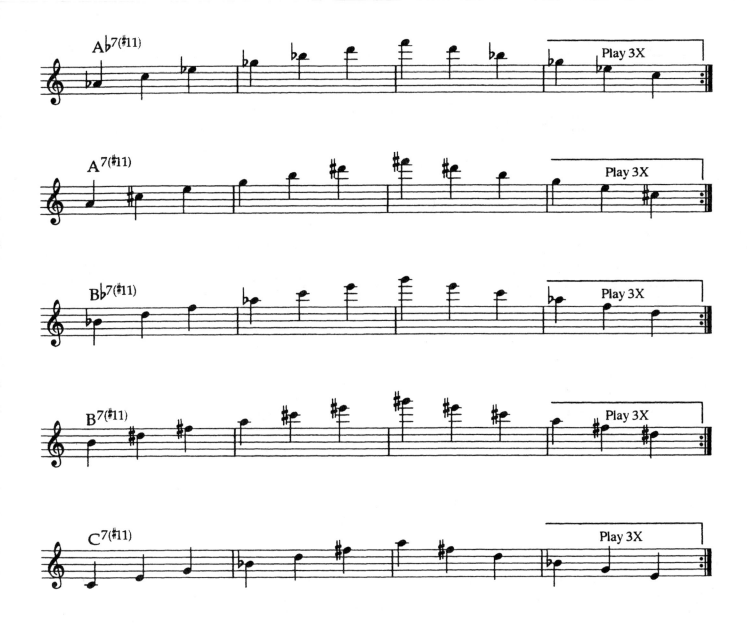

DOUBLE DIMINISHED SCALES

DOUBLE DIMINISHED SCALE EXERCISE

DOUBLE DIMINISHED CHORD EXERCISE

Right hand plays two notes of C diminished 7.

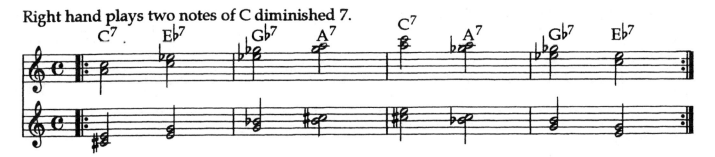

Left hand plays two notes of C# diminished 7.

Right hand plays two notes of Db diminished 7.

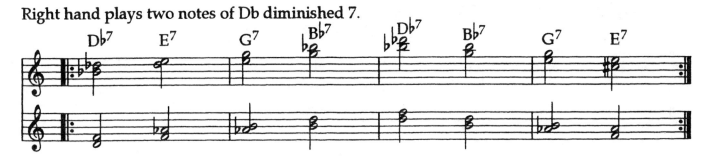

Left hand plays two notes of D diminished 7.

Right hand plays two notes of D diminished 7.

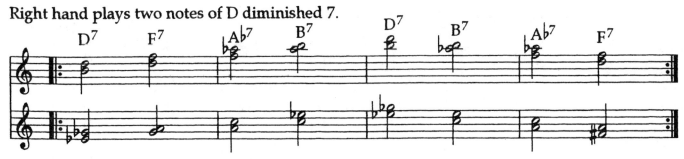

Left hand plays two notes of Eb diminished 7.

DOUBLE DIMINISHED CHORD EXERCISE

Right hand plays two notes of C diminished 7.

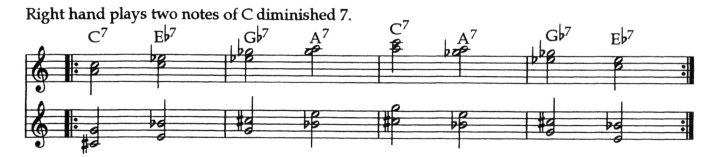

Left hand plays two notes of C# diminished 7.

Right hand plays two notes of Db diminished 7.

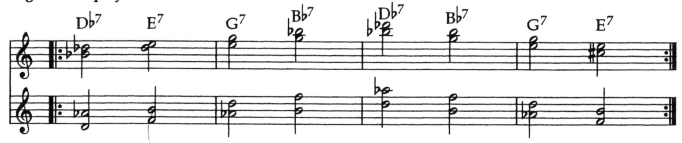

Left hand plays two notes of D diminished 7.

Right hand plays two notes of D diminished 7.

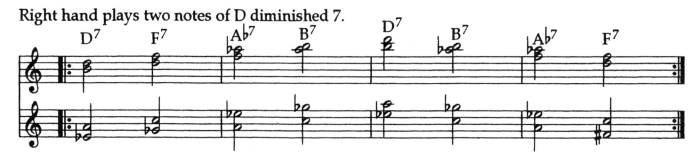

Left hand plays two notes of Eb diminished 7.

DOUBLE DIMINISHED CHORD EXERCISE

Right hand plays two notes of C diminished 7.

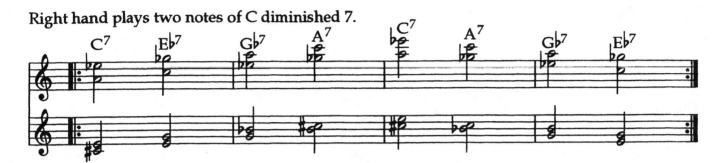

Left hand plays two notes of C# diminished 7.

Right hand plays two notes of Db diminished 7.

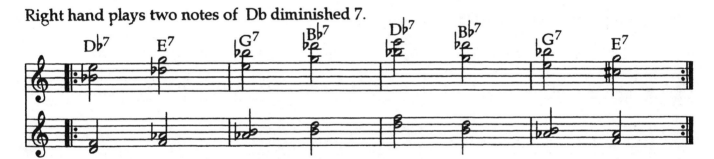

Left hand plays two notes of D diminished 7.

Right hand plays two notes of D diminished 7.

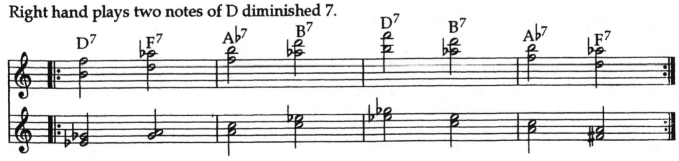

Left hand plays two notes of Eb diminished 7.

DOUBLE DIMINISHED CHORD EXERCISE

Right hand plays two notes of C diminished 7.

Left hand plays two notes of C# diminished 7.

Right hand plays two notes of Db diminished 7.

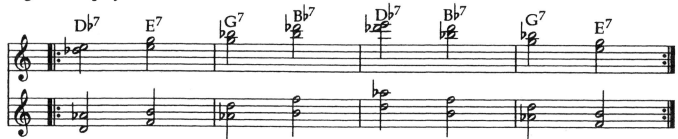

Left hand plays two notes of D diminished 7.

Right hand plays two notes of D diminished 7.

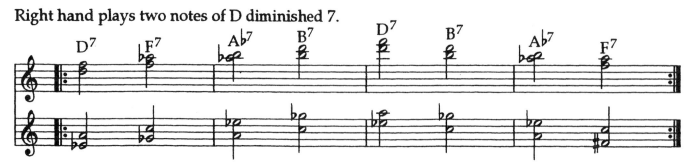

Left hand plays two notes of Eb diminished 7.

46

DOUBLE DIMINISHED CHORD EXERCISE

Right hand plays two notes of C diminished 7.

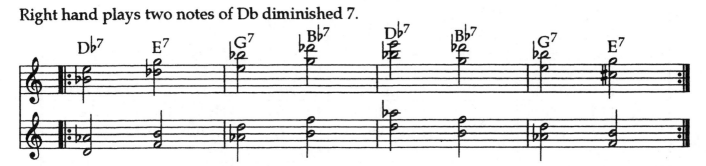

Left hand plays two notes of C# diminished 7.

Right hand plays two notes of Db diminished 7.

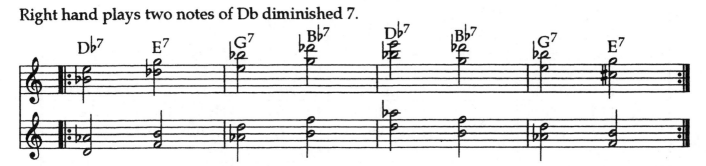

Left hand plays two notes of D diminished 7.

Right hand plays two notes of D diminished 7.

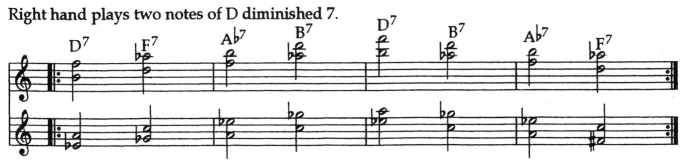

Left hand plays two notes of Eb diminished 7.

REHARMONIZATION CHART
C–F

Note:	C	C#	D	Eb	E	F
1	C	C#	D	Eb	E	F
2	Bb	B	C	Db	D	Eb
3	Am	Bbm	Bm	Cm	C#m	Dm
3	AbM	AM	BbM	BM	CM	DbM
4	G7sus4	Ab7sus4	A7sus4	Bb7sus4	B7sus4	C7sus4
5	F#7(b5)	G7(b5)	Ab7(b5)	A7(b5)	Bb7(b5)	B7(b5)
5	F#m7(b5)	Gm7(b5)	Abm7(b5)	Am7(b5)	Bbm7(b5)	Bm7(b5)
5	FM	F#M	GM	AbM	AM	BbM
5	E+7	F+7	Gb+7	G+7	Ab+7	A+7
6	Eb6	E6	F6	Gb6	G6	Ab6
6	Ebm6	Em6	Fm6	Gbm6	Gm6	Abm6
7	Ebdim7	Edim7	Fdim7	Gbdim7	Gdim7	Abdim7
7	D7	Eb7	E7	F7	F#7	G7
7	Dm7	Ebm7	Em7	Fm7	F#m7	Gm7
7	Dm7(b5)	Ebm7(b5)	Em7(b5)	Fm7(b5)	F#m7(b5)	Gm7(b5)
7	Dm7(#5)	Ebm7(#5)	Em7(#5)	Fm7(#5)	F#m7(#5)	Gm7(#5)
7	DbM7	DM7	EbM7	EM7	FM7	F#M7
7	DbM7(b3)	DM7(b3)	EbM7(b3)	EM7(b3)	FM7(b3)	F#M7(b3)
7	DbM7(#5)	DM7(#5)	EbM7(#5)	EM7(#5)	FM7(#5)	F3M7(#5)
9	B7(b9)	C7(b9)	Db7(b9)	D7(b9)	Eb7(b9)	E7(b9)
9	Bb9	B9	C9	Db9	D9	Eb9
9	Bb6/9	B6/9	C6/9	Db6/9	D6/9	Eb6/9
9	Bbm6/9	Bm6/9	Cm6/9	Dbm6/9	Dm6/9	Ebm6/9
9	BbM9	BM9	CM9	DbM9	DM9	EbM9
9	Bbm9	Bm9	Cm9	Dbm9	Dm9	Ebm9
9	A7#9	Bb7(#9)	B7(#9)	C7(#9)	Db7(#9)	D7(#9)
11	Gm11	Abm11	Am11	Bbm11	Bm11	Cm11
11	Gb9+11	G9+11	Ab9+11	A9+11	Bb9+11	B9+11
11	GbM9+11	GM9+11	AbM9+11	AM9+11	BbM9+11	BM9+11
13	Eb13	E13	F13	F#13	G13	Ab13